Books by John Marohn

Tiorunda Stories (2008)

Recovery Journey (2012)

Book I
Beginnings

Book II
Psychological & Spiritual Issues

Book III
Philosophical & Cultural Issues

All books are available on Kindle

Poems From An Old Guy

John Marohn

Beaufleuve Publishing

PO Box 498

Buffalo, New York 14207

ISBN: 978-0-9796961-5-2   0-9796961-5-1

Dedicated to John and Amy

Table of Contents

Your Breath Has Many Colors

Your breath has many colors,
Brown, certain and firm,
Like the park tree
I saw yesterday
On my morning walk,
Sometimes too sure
Of itself, if you ask me.

But, then again, your breath turns pink,
Lightheaded, forgetful
As my grandmother,
Who once found her teeth
In the trunk of her car.

You've been known
To go all red on me,
Screaming as obvious
As the blazing sun
I can see out our
Window this morning.

Then swooning into
Your violet breath,
All sensual and elegant
After your third glass
Of Dom Perignon,
Asking me if God
Lives in both of your breasts
Or just favors one.

Your green breath is my favorite,
For it is the grass
Where I can rest my old naked body
On a summer afternoon in July
When we're halfway through
The plans we stopped making
A long time ago.

Imaginé

She was silent today, another dry event,
Trying to train herself into the habit
Of not thinking about him,
But feeling the cool memory
That lingered in between
The cars she passed on the Interstate
Driving to the summer cottage
On a winter weekend
To sit quietly inside his absence,
Opening empty cupboards,
Breaking frozen branches,
Scouring the floor with her iPhone light
To find the small notes he left her
During the week, his monk's notices
Of celibate days not working for him,
But promising to let go
If she would make her truce
To surrender quietly to his words
Until, according to the contract,
He would leave her small blank pages.
"My robin's wounds," he texted her.

William Pitt, My Blind Grandfather

He was blind, his eyes suffocated

Into silence,

In his grief, imagining

His body's stark opposition to

The innocent flow

Of children in bow ties

And full pink skirts,

Or an aging oak's

Craggy shreds of skin,

Once seen by the

Boy he used to be,

Eyes wide open,

Squinting against

An orgy of sun

His pupils knew

Could not absorb.

But now, in old age,

His eyes cannot remember

What they didn't see yesterday,

Austere, naked, burglarized by time,

Bargaining with his body

To hear more than he could endure.

And So Forth

She imagined Harry one more time

Standing in front

Of the kitchen sink

Using that old

Green wet sponge

To scrape the hardened

Toast crumbs and bits of

Scrambled eggs from

Their morning plates,

Gently filing the plates

Into the dishwasher,

"The ritual of the banal,"

He used to call it,

In her mind,

The pattern of security

She could count on,

Like the cold nose

Of their German Shepherd,

Eli, they put down

Last winter,

Or the memory

Of Harry's cold toes

Rubbing against the back

Of her feet at

Three in the morning

When she would hear the

Usual train whistle

From the tracks

On Blanchard Street.

Things That Never Were

He learned as a child
To be silent,
Remembering events to recall
On buses and trains,
Or as a passenger
On a long car trip
In his monk's space
Of reverie for things
That never were:
A mother who spoke garlands,
A father who felt grief,
Brothers who knew themselves,
Nuns who had last names,
A host that bled
On his first-communion suit
To let him know
That redemption was real—
All repackaged in the odor
Of things wished for.

Tit For Tat

He had stopped talking to his wife

In the mornings,

Knowing she had descended

Into the crudity of desire

And cheap romance

With another man,

Occasions he had refined

As a free-lancer

Into quiet affairs

Of little substance

And no return calls,

While she looked

For something more

Than holding his hand

At a hockey game,

Some permanent vine

In their relationship

That had grown to stay,

A gift that would

Melt the chill

Of his decision

To stop loving her

Sometime last April

When the moon smiled

At their youngest child,

Now a young adult,

Slamming the front door

For the last time.

Nada

He couldn't comprehend
Nothing existing
Before the one moment
When everything began
In its wild chaotic unfurling.

Nothing, complete absence,
Silence, not even
A sweet chance at expectation,
Like leaning over the curb
To look for the next bus.
Or fear, opening up the door
For another look
At a week-old baby,
Distrustful that such
A small life could endure.

Maybe Yesterday

Maybe yesterday or the day before,

He walked across the room

In his usual way, shoulders straight,

His lean face

Convinced it had solved

Last year's debt that hit

Them like a late August thunderstorm.

He kept dreaming of horses,

Their sleek curved backs

In the afternoon sun,

Seducing him into more

Credit cards in

Leather wallets filled

With lottery tickets

And round-trip tickets

To Las Vegas.

"Business trips," he called them,

Slips of paper with phone numbers,

An endless array of names—

Valery, indigo, Sherry, Bubbles,

On the back of Marriott Inn cards

His wife found in the bathroom

Waste paper basket.

Fidelity, a memory to be forgotten,

His wife hanging on to loyalty,

The more compelling argument

Like a long, slow spring rain

That would sink in deep

And last until the next year.

The End

She folded the napkins into a cardboard box

Knowing that this was really the last time

She would say to herself, "this"

Would be "the last time"

She would ever move.

Steadiness, the constant

She survived on,

Like a two-year-old

Crawling to the bedroom window

Every morning to see

A neighbor's dog,

Or the postman

Arriving at one in the afternoon,

Or an old French film

That would whisper

To her snoring husband,

"Fin."

She Missed His Funeral Yesterday

She missed his funeral yesterday
Not convinced she could gather
Enough solid grief
To moor her steadily
Into wanting to
Remember him.

But then again
They were married
For a time
When the earth,
By his own admission,
Did not move
Beyond its dry rituals
Of undizzying speed
And long corridors.

She read his obituary,
Sufficient in its dullness
Of names pulled from
The family files—
Mary, George, Anna,

Siblings who died,
She was told,
From boredom
And unweeded gardens.
Eric, Vince, Julia—
The children
Who left their nest,
Grateful to breathe
Their own air.

She continues
To cross-reference him,
Hoping in the end
That some bleak category
Will open a rusted charm
She gratefully missed.

God's Imaginings

In the arched beams
Of sacramental wood,
God feels
The steady stream of the willing,
Not the rubber band
Figures, bent, slouched
Along urine-smelling corridors,
Frail doilies
Of their former selves,
Slouched in their dumb memories
Of medicine-cabinet doors
Aching in their hesitancy
To speak of cures,
Doubtful anodynes
Against the curse
Of what He
Forgets to heal.

Quickening

God, the nuns told us,
Quickened our bodies with souls,
A nervous process among those
Accustomed to flaws and early mistakes,
The body unwilling to hide
From its own thighs
And the honest odors
Of backyard barbecues.

"Imagine," Sister Gabriel said in fourth grade,
"God injecting an anchor
Inside our bodies, an anchor
That grounds us to the sweetness
Of His grace. That anchor
Is our everlasting soul. That's what
'Quickening' is, class."

Gerry Hill, with a keen ear
And a fast mouth, raised his hand
"What does 'everlasting' mean, Sister?"
"It means your soul will live forever, Gerry,
Even though your body will die."

"Does the soul get any quicker in heaven, Sister"?
"No, Gerry, it just keeps pace."

Gerry kept looking at Marjorie's
Bare feet curled under the desk,
Her shoes and socks
Pushed next to the radiator
That ticked and hummed
Into the sunless afternoon.

Life and Death

They had been together
For sixty years,
The silences friendlier
Than they used to be.
He sold car insurance,
Learning early in his career
That liability always rubbed
Against the possibility of death,
A limited reward for staying alive,
Breathing the air the rest of us do.
She worked at the gas company,
Listening for thirty years
To frantic customers
Calling in when they
Suspected gas leaks,
Later discovering what odors could shift
From her father's backyard roses
And her mother's lingering cologne,
To compete in silence
Against her breath's final exit.

Dido

The natural flavor of your indignation
Melted into silence,
Forcing you to choose
The darkest splinter of your grief
For the man who succumbed
So readily, as men do,
To some mythical plan
To make themselves heroes
Of another country,
While you, in your inevitable pose,
Wander in your own madness,
Your dark hair battling the wind,
Running through the courtyard,
Screaming at hungry dogs
And dazed cats,
Planning to reinvent yourself,
Without much luck,
From open-thighed lover
To a quaint painting of
The courtesan you once were
To show to your grandchildren.

Primal Fear

He had the primal fear
That life would just evaporate into
Elemental emptiness,
Disappearing, like a numb rabbit,
Into a magician's hat.

Not the cat's indifferent withdrawal
Behind the sofa,
Asserting its fatigue
With the scrappy world
That offered nothing more
Than a can of tuna
And a hand's sweep
Down its tolerating back.

But a shaking zero
That could neither add
A cent to itself
To give it some worth,
Nor subtract a dollar
To make it less attractive.

Moksha

Irene looked out the bedroom window
At the breeze exhaling
Its frantic breath
Through backyard trees,
Leaves, like nervous
Bristles on a paint brush,
In a mad rush to finish
Another clumsy scene,
A cradle's fast rocking
To the aching pulse of
Of her second month
Without work.

The restlessness of
Nothing to do,
Her mind rambling
Through stammering resentments
Of being too old,
Age arriving without warning
Or a reservation,
Legs hesitant to finish a stride,
Release denied, payments overdue,

The sun descending
Like a tired old bull
To its sparse den.

It Was There

And it was there,
An unshaven memory
Of a worn path
Along the canal,
Of a tall, thin
Young woman,
Let's say, for the record,
Around 18, blond hair,
A school uniform,
A chemistry book,
A lunch bag,
Waiting for the mystery
To be revealed,
Willing to stop like a faun,
Darting nose to the ground,
But trained for centuries
To look up, a habit
Of keen survival,
Hearing her first cello,
Which wept a song
She would hum
Between classes.

Never Enough

You told me I gave you no room,
When I know
The world is never ample,
It can always be fuller
Than its plain self,
More pregnant with each month,
The expanse of fresh geese
Breathing out more fullness
On the belly of the sky.

And I, in this ever widening circle,
Why can't I choose
To decide when the water's edge
Is not enough?
Or stop at your satiety,
The brim of whatever
Is enough for you?
I will not wait
For your self-defined limit.
I will move to test your endurance
To open your body, gently
To a new surrender.

Rubber Band Day

She had smiled again,
Quizzically, at first, her head bent
In its usual angle of confusion,
Certain that her job was safe.

For no particular reason,
Her boyfriend surrendered
His half naked body
To a gaggle of groping hands
Lifting him into a tub of water,
The warmth of his epiphany
Tasting like slivers of hot glass
On her abandoned tongue.

Her grandfather was scheduled for surgery
On Saturday, his left carotid
Ninety percent blocked,
Her cousin pregnant by
The lead actor in a theater group
That came to town
For a two-night performance
Of Oedipus Rex.

Gone Before Bedtime

Cassius was thirteen, walking lithely
Along a country road in Alabama
With the moon's approval.

Two white boys strolling
On the sidewalk on their
Way to the other end of town
Bored in their fatigue,
The summer's end
Refusing comfort
For their tedium
As they listened
To a frog's last gasp
Along the river's bank,
The night not available
To harass,
The grass too weak to battle
In August.

In the white boys' movie,
One stranger left
To put up a fight,

Arrogant in his joy,
Smiling into emptiness
For no good reason.

A fast scuffle before
A jealous lover's chokehold,
Three blows to the stomach
Like an anvil against hard steel,
History's return to avenge
A black boy's last breath,
Arms melting, legs collapsing,
Memories swept off the earth,
Amnesia resurrected in a
Slumped body thrown into a
River's murmuring current.

I'll Fly Away

These mornings had more promise
Than the ones she slept through
Last year.

Today an old hymn
In her head,
"I'll fly away in the morning
When I die"

Yes, transport herself
Through the rubble
Of another chemo treatment
With her husband, her pinochle companion,
And Friday night fish fries.
She, still refusing to be confused
By road maps,
Held a steady wheel
And a firm accelerator
On the way to Toronto,
Always ready for a stop
At a Tim Horton's.

A gentle woman with
Solid gray hair, blue eyes,
A torso that came alive
Years ago on a gurney
And a doctor's promise
Of a few more years,
Gliding past sunsets
With a solid pulse.

Le Corps

The body moves through
Corridors of forgetfulness,
Energized in youth
By summer risks
And winter hazards.

In adolescence, posing
More than once
In front of risky mirrors
To screen for blemishes
Of self-loathing.

Early adulthood whispering to these limbs,
"You will last forever,"
Before doubts in middle age
When tubes of blood announce
The avenging family genes.

Modern old age, the victor
Against ancient fatalities
And early deaths,
Prolonging time and easy forgetting.

Coup d'oeil

I saw you today,

You looked quickly, a second's glance,

Window shopping,

Thinking in intervals,

Broken fragments of glass

On the floor of a seedy bar.

And I, returning the glance,

Preparing Romeo's soliloquy,

An altar full of clergy,

A best man, a rented tux,

Central Park, Proust,

A dark sonnet,

A family health insurance plan

With no deductible.

Again

A kettle whistling on the stove,
Its voice rushed to the untrained ear,
But to this old habit of a man,
A purring of the familiar,
This hissing welcome to the feast
Of the sun's surprises.

In this hymn of the known
Is to hear your soft feet upon the floor,
Your body moving to its own rhythm,
Your head on my aging shoulders,
Your night's sweet whisper
Melting my desire for any new gifts,
Except this day and an album of you.

18th Century Garden

The universe was organized
And well thought out,
Everything in its proper place,
The rain arriving at the moment
The crocus and hyacinth
Leaned into the sky,
Like winter lovers banished
Into silence and now smiling
For the return of the familiar,
The sun placed at intervals
To mark the time
Between the ache of arctic loss
And the laughter of lush green
Along the bush-filled paths,
Late summer waiting with a dry mouth
And the closing in of night.

Favorite Things

He liked cats,
A much better investment
Than friends
Who were always late,
Or arguing about global warming,
Team scores, politicians.

Cats knew when to eat,
Avoided eye contact
Unless there was a benefit,
A fear, rejection,
The only three reasons
For staying on the planet.

Cats knew where to hide,
Something he had never learned
When his parents stumbled
In drunk on Friday nights
Fighting about
Other lovers and nursing homes.

Cats went under beds,

Curled up on couches,
Wandered in circles
In the kitchen after school,
Whining for food or attention.

Human debates and complaints
Seemed useless,
A bother spun into meaning,
Never forgotten, revisited,
Not in ritual, but in desire
To hold on, for letting go
Simply meant there was
Nothing more to say.

He was fine with that.

#MeToo

Something still wasn't right,
The microwave worked
To warm another cup of coffee
After her usual shower
Before she went to work.

All the windows opened easily,
The morning newspaper
Resting undisturbed in its
Cellophane wrapper
On the kitchen table.

Light snow sifted its way
Through the air,
The morning light unwilling
To arrive yet to the world,
And she, afraid to admit
Any hope for her sister in Montana,
The poet who spoke too tenderly
Of the forced gifts
They both surrendered as teenagers,
Their bodies, like weeping violins

In an empty concert hall,

Each losing interest

In being surprised at anything.

Ohio Born

I am thinking about my father tonight,
Ohio-born in crevices of stern Lutherans
Packaging their desires
For a later time
When some would leave
The summer night's fireflies
And the smell of hay
Or move to another part of town
That had a public pool.

Conversations were slim:
About firecrackers,
Two drunk uncles,
Chinese porno cards,
And grandmother's pregnancy
Before she met my grandfather.

The steady fires of Hell
Were never discussed
And Heaven, a Sunday word,
Out of the realm
Of possibility for the

Housewives and railroad men

Who knew the hymns

But lived their lives

Here and forever.

Friday Fantasy

Today's list of possible lovers:
One group estranged from the ordinary,
Bored by laundromats,
Intrigued by subtitles and coffee shops,
The practical invested in shift work,
Netflix streamers, Verizon badgers,
Gentle lemmings out for
Sunday walks in the park,
Foreigners back from Prague,
Joggers, Francophiles,
Solitary commuters,
Or just you, naked,
Showered in your soft skin,
Poems falling from your blue eyes.

The Moon

It is round

It arrives

It shines

It reflects

It is the sun's stepchild

It comes out

It stares without blinking

It draws us to it

It approves

It hangs out in cemeteries

It sometimes sleeps in a cradle

It watches without judgment

It hides

It is silent

It is still

It waits for brides to stop dancing

It wonders

It is the desert's flashlight

It is the night's open eye

It sleeps

It whispers to werewolves

and drunks

It blushes

It caresses schizophrenics

It permits

It reveals

It sings the same song to all

first-time lovers

It cannot hear politicians

It stays when relatives leave

It holds the gun to your head

Makes incisions that don't hurt

It grieves like an old man

It cries for limping dogs

It is never jealous of your friends

It won't say goodbye.

I Am Old

I am old.
In my brief certainties,
Destined to short debates
And stained toilets
Once brazenly clean.
I am a one-pair-of-shoes guy
With lazy underwear,
Two missing combs,
Ivy-growing nose hairs,
Mounds of pills in orange tubes,
Toenails hard as turtle shells.
My ties are too wide.
I cough at movies.
My body slides out of chairs,
Reluctantly. My pen hesitates.
Headlines will do for today.
Television shadows invade
My bedroom.
My mind wanders
Into my father's garden
Or into the basement
As I hear his fingers

Rattling through

His tool box.

Abandonment

His mother left him when he was a child,
Would she exit again in another form,
In all the lovers he scrapped
For hanging around too long,
Too restrained in their passion,
Or clinging like an abused dog?

Tragedy would wrap its arms around him
On days when the sun offered solace,
Possibility escaping him every day
As his new friend leasing out
Only the bad news, his best seller.

Someone dying in the last act
His favorite ending,
Comedy, the stepchild of a
Tired joke.

Here Today

She could not be more herself today,
A simple woman of vetted tastes,
After two romances she hurled herself into
On the Cape last summer.

One a concert pianist choosing
To fan himself with the rhythms
Of another century,
The other, a plumber,
Who counted errors
In copper and flushed toilets.

She would settle this fall
For an old poet
Dizzying her with words
That would dance and sting
On the flower of who she once was
In the steady arc
Of a young lover's interest.

Vive La Différence

That gap existing between the strains
Of who we are or wish to be,
You wanting to be as still
As a twelve wheeler
Out of gas on the Interstate
In a blizzard,
Me in the large craving
To be heard
Explaining the plot of
Just another story
Someone else wrote,
A second edition
That improved upon nothing
To begin with.

Suboxone

My lovely agonist,
Cruel substitute,
Halloween mask,
Candied-apple Lover
In your cheap eye-liner,
I want to lust for you
As my first drop-dead date
In concrete basements.
But you were sent
By some official
In green pants
With a name tag
And ugly shoes
I cannot trust
Right now.

But give me time.
For I need a lover,
As young hearts do,
Some shiny face
That doesn't nod off
And eyes that don't close,

And long-fingered hands

On piano keys

On a Sunday afternoon.

Ménage

A third person cannot
Do what two have found
As the right length of a kiss,
Tertiary tongues spoiling
The settled contracts
Of imperfection
That cannot be made whole
By an intruder's adrenaline,
The huckster's offer
Of more dazzling fruit
Rotting in its excess.

An Aging God

Grace, a gift for the unworthy
From an unknown lover
Bartering as young gods always do
For more than respect,
Rejecting the cordiality
Of statesmen and underpaid doormen.
Who is this gift-giver, this once bronze god
Fermented into an old man's unsteadiness,
Weak ankles, aching knee-caps, a lazy mouth?
Generosity cannot shuttle out of the arms
Of aging gods smoking cigars, one unsteady hand
Guiding a wheeled walker through the halls
Of the soundless stalks of the unrepentant.

Six of One

Actor he always was,
Wheelchairing his way
Into his impoverished look,
Pants with empty pockets,
Thin, liver-spotted hands,
Dry feet, hair coarse
As a horse rope,
Eyes duller than
An over-used kitchen knife.
He will recall
The stone bridge
Over the village creek
Where she chose
To feel the fever
He said started
As soon as he
Walked out the door
Of his summer cottage
To meet her every August.

"It was never enough.
Like a bowl full of fruit,

When all the kids were home,"
He said.
But she never told him
It was sufficient,
Like today, when
she made another choice
To see him briefly
And leave him
To over-smiling nurses
And the sad odor of urine.

Margret

He's done this before even on his methodical days,
Pills aligned on the cupboard,
Morning talk shows, the chattering bells
Of actors hawking one more film
Over toast and curled eggs.
What had he forgotten again
In the hollow cave of his dreams?
The rent, the electric, cable?
No, something else, a sliver event
Impaled in his memory.
Tom's wake?
No, that was in January,
The fifteenth, to be exact,
When he ran out of toilet paper
And Miracle Whip.
Maybe Margret, inevitable Margret,
Who lived downstairs and showered
Every day at five-thirty in the morning,
Returning for a guest visit at eight,
To wander through her forgotten crevices.

Margret. Damn. Margret.

What was it? A movie? Lunch?

He paused. Now he remembered.

Vomiting Margret, sun-bald,

Pencil-thin, frail as his mother's voice,

Ten-o'clock-appointment Margret

In her cabaret wig and slim high heels.

He tied his shoes.

Transgendered Me

Swimming against
The orders
Of others
To be
Who I am not,
Body parts
From my mother's womb,
Gifted back
To the cruel source
Who made me
What I never was,
The old world's contract
Broken by my
Own stern will,
Penis as memory
Vagina as hope,
Breasts blossoming
From my chest,
Hair shaven
From my bony legs,
Communion miracle,
The old host

Disappearing

Into new flesh

And flowing blood

Of this, the

Newly honed

And tender me.

The Balance

She had loved him
All these years
Played out in dreams
Of reaching up for
Ripe plums rotting
At the touch of her
Pinched fingers,
In competition
With her closed eyelids
On other nights
That hid redeeming stories
Of a young man
Who read Virgil and Molière,
Who could slide his tongue
Along the ridge of her neck
Emptying the vessel of
Who she thought she was
To fill it with the sheer sheen
Of possibility.

The Old School

He had wallpapered rooms
When the urge moved him,
Sandpapered the paint off radiators
Even in the attic,
Dismantled the old lawn mower
In the garage, the second one
His oldest son had hidden
Behind the boxes filled
With books on the Civil War.
A fresh coat of paint
Could hide a memory
Annihilate the worn and the tired.
A leaking faucet annoyed him
Like the tapping feet
Of a squirrel on attic beams,
Putty, the "magic herb"
That "could seal up any hole"
He was fond of saying
At the dinner table
When the conversation
Got too deep.

He repaired, painted, wired,
Sawed, shoveled, piled, planted.
He never shared his dreams
With his wife or kids—
Old mattresses on the curb,
Refrigerators, bathtubs, sinks,
Sofas, random pillows, screens,
Broken windows, carburetors,
Spark plugs, rusted mufflers.
"The old school" his brother said
Of him at the wake.

Before and After

Patient death can arrive

In the afternoon mail,

Never looked for

Like a phone bill,

But in a letter from

A dying friend

He hadn't seen

In twenty years,

The one who took

His former girlfriend

To the senior prom,

Married her three years later,

And had three kids

With ordinary names,

Who all went

To small Methodist colleges

In the Midwest

Where the corn

Never stopped growing.

Credo

Yesterday he was asked
What he believes in
As if the broken cliffs
Along the sea
When the fog
Rolls in aren't enough
Or the children faking fear
Running through a sprinkler.

Trucks and buses
Make wide turns,
Two-year-olds
Scream in restaurants,
Umbrellas are useless
In a windstorm,
A one-month-old
Doesn't choose
Which nipple is more tender,
The sky takes in any fool's eyes.

Its Green Self

She had been on the farm,
By her recollection,
For forty years,
The fences looking more
Scorched and tired
Than they did yesterday.
The barn tilting to the east
Drawn by the morning's hope,
The two cows she saw
Through the kitchen window
Looking disgusted by time's apathy
But deciding to wait it out,
And she in her morning jeans
Imagining the grass returning
To its former green self.

The Other Option

He was asked to write
A love poem,
Not about cemeteries
And frogless ponds
Their darkness weighing in
On lives used to
Commuter drives,
Passing lanes,
Parking ramps,
Slammed car doors,
Disgruntled bosses,
Hurried lunches,
Iphones that Counted
Seconds in secret.

Rather, an apparition
Arriving like a late train
Right before closing time,
Of a young woman,
Shy, with uneven teeth,
Small breasts,
A scientist's hands,

Walking across the hill,

The seduction of innocence

Speaking to him

Of poems, earnest questions,

Beach blankets and novels,

Of women torn

Between men who dreamed

And men whose bank accounts

Were always full.

A Boy With Huntington's

I was afraid for you
As you twisted your face
With your cupped hands,
Your right foot jabbing
The bystanding wall.
Arguing with the opposing day,
You said your dervish prayers
To Shiva of the dancing arms
To stay your frantic legs
And thighs buzzing like bees
In a lidded jar.
How would I hold you
In sweet contentment?

After, in your feathery calm,
You were like a lazy lizard
Sleeping on drift wood
Or a string snapped from a shoe
Laying limp on a wood floor.
Too tired to talk
As you gazed into the

Summer glaze of daffodils

And castles along the Hudson River,

Watching impish, howling cats

And two frantic squirrels

Darting across telephone lines,

One running from love.

Teenager's First Date

Showing up on time
Is the easy part.
The dashboard of
His rented car
Free of dust,
Wax-clean,
Vacuumed carpets
And a lemon-smelling
Tag dangling from
The rear view mirror.
One more look
In the sun-visor
Mirror, an angled glance
At the straggly sideburns.
Fly firmly zipped.
Spitting on his closed
Index fingers,
He drags them along
The creases of
His black pants.

He pulls out a hanky

To shine the tips

Of his eager shoes.

Gently tugging

The bottom of his red tie,

He firmly wrestles

With the knot

To shield the

Top button from

Strangers looking

For flaws.

He opens his sport coat,

Tilting his nose

Into the dark corners

Of both armpits.

He turns off the ignition,

Opens the door,

And looks up at

The scoop of a moon

Glancing down at

The familiar.

Je Me Souviens

I remember you once,
Your nut-flavored hair
Jostled by my hands
Sliding to your
Bare shoulders,
Straps falling like
Patient rain,
Rumpled silk and lace
Descending to the willing floor,
The sweet summer melon
And hive-dripping honey
In the soundless flesh
Of my desire.

Another One-Night Stand

Meeting under the shoals of

Silent blankets,

We hear a simmering

Gideon from a motel drawer,

Whispering warnings

Of scalded souls

Writhing in regret.

We, after all,

Require infidelity to a fault,

Staggering in the rinks

Of our desires,

Baffled at the world's indifference.

C'est Fini

You chose last night
To end your gaunt battle
Against life's oblivion,
Deciding to have your neck
Bear the burden
Of your solitude
In a quiet cellar,
Your pallbearers
A silent furnace,
A tool box,
A folded lawn chair,
Three unmatched socks,
Your father's charcoaled
Portrait against the humid wall
Gazing at your dangling body,
His affirmation
That all things end.

The Other Woman

Concubined into silent lunches
And ardent price tags,
I come to you
As I always do,
In the dying heat
Of one more fall.

I am the new addition to your house,
The extra winter scarf,
The second pair of
Comfortable shoes.
You, my sweet occasion,
The odor of vacuumed rugs
In air-conditioned motel rooms
Still lingering on my bald feet.
You, the choice I always make
To commit once again
To another fatal season.

Rumor Has It

No one in town
Knew their last names,
They lived in a
One-room log cabin
With no electricity,
Up on the ridge
Behind two willows
And five fifteen-foot
Blue spruces.
Rumors painted them
As brother and sister
In a witness protection program,
Lovers tired of New York City,
An excommunicated nun and priest.
Johnny Bedford saw two copies
Of Plato in the back seat
Of their ten-year-old
Ford station wagon
Parked in front of Woolworth's.

The woman seemed to enjoy
Browsing in the New Fiction section

Of the library,

Her partner wandering off

Into Medieval History

And science journals,

Leading the rest of us to guess

If he satisfied her at night

Or if he had some

Weird torture machines

Below ground level

Underneath a secret trap door

Covered with pictures of Galileo

And his favorite Papal encyclicals.

"What do you do with your time?"

A mother once asked her son

In late August.

We were all too young then

To answer with conviction.

But now, well,

Much the same stuff:

Gather information,

Think of things to say

To parents and teenagers,

Check out houses,

Back seats of cars,
Wonder if any husband
Is who he says he is.

A Second Version

Jake once told a friend
The lake was east of the gas station,
Across from the drug store;
Every eight-year-old knew
It was west of the candy store
Near the post office.
In a conversation with a minister
At a going-away party
For his sister
He made up the name
Of his dog.
After a hockey game,
Driving home,
He told his brother
He had black lung disease,
Got three women pregnant
In two upstate counties,
Was on his third novel.
When he was four,
He remembered his mother
Telling him he didn't
Have the luxury

To take his time to get up

Or go to bed.

He decided then,

Stories could always use

A second version.

An Old Man's Company

At sixteen, he remembered
She was once there,
When inkwells were invented
To dip stabs of memory into
To record her slim walk,
A faded geometry book,
A blue dotted head scarf,
A small black square purse
Hanging from two leather straps,
An overly bleached white blouse.

Seventy years later,
An ancient desire relit in hospice,
An unshaven old man dreaming
Through steady breaths
Of a tall girl with long blond hair
Opening a metal door
Into a small chapel,
Leading him to an altar
Full of burning candles
And red roses,
Oaths made,

A quick exit to a hospital

The wet wrinkled skin of a child,

Wallpaper bunnies, swings,

Summers in the Adirondacks

Nurtured secrets forgotten,

Diplomas wrapped in blue ribbons,

Cremated fathers,

Mothers wheeled into nursing homes,

And then

Air stolen in the night

By naked thieves

Lonely for an old man's company.

Blessed Fault

I often fool myself into sanctity,

The credo of the stainless,

That whistles tenderly in the morning,

Hastening my giant strides of will.

But I am less inclined to virtue

When I am presented a complete score

Of innocence, every instrument allocated

Its brief moment of holy affirmation

In old, familiar bowdlerized tunes.

Perfection will just not do,

No matter how lovely the rose's odor

Or the fresh lips of my last lover,

For catastrophes draw me more into

The ragged corner of my undoing,

Where the tilted ground

Of my uncertain heart

Is scorched a tender shade,

Bruised back into possibility.

It is there among the culpable

That I pray to live out my days.

Mise en Scène

A swing in a park snaps at its height,
A child with gray eyes
And bruised knees
Drops to the hard earth,
Mudslides slip into a Portland road
Surprising a farmer and his wife,
A bridge collapses
In Milwaukee
At four in the afternoon,
A lawyer,
A maintenance worker,
An electrician,
A neurosurgeon,
Still missing,
Absence the harsher pain,
The possibility of return
Ringing in the mind,
Like a banging door
On an empty cabin door
In the middle of winter.

John Marohn is an author who hails from Buffalo, New York. He has written one novel, *Tiorunda Stories,* and three books on alcohol recovery.

Poems From an Old Guy is his first collection of poems.

Made in the USA
Middletown, DE
27 May 2019